Lancaster County, Pennsylvania, Postcards

Featuring the Collection of the Landis Valley Museum

Irwin Richman

Schiffer Publishing Ltd
4880 Lower Valley Road, Atglen, PA 19310

Other Schiffer Books by Irwin Richman:
PennsylvanianGerman Arts (2001)
German Architecture in America (2003)
Pennsylvania German Farms, Gardens and Seeds (2007)
Seed Art (2008)

Library of Congress Control Number: 2008921384

Designed by John P. Cheek
Cover design by Bruce Waters
Type set in Birch/Zurich BT

ISBN:978-0-7643-2970-8
Printed in China

Published by Schiffer Publishing Ltd.
4880 Lower Valley Road
Atglen, PA 19310
Phone: (610) 593-1777; Fax: (610) 593-2002
E-mail: Info@schifferbooks.com

For the largest selection of fine reference books on this and related subjects, please visit our web site at **www.schifferbooks.com**
We are always looking for people to write books on new and related subjects. If you have an idea for a book please contact us at the above address.

This book may be purchased from the publisher.
Include $3.95 for shipping.
Please try your bookstore first.
You may write for a free catalog.

In Europe, Schiffer books are distributed by
Bushwood Books
6 Marksbury Ave.
Kew Gardens
Surrey TW9 4JF England
Phone: 44 (0) 20 8392-8585; Fax: 44 (0) 20 8392-9876
E-mail: info@bushwoodbooks.co.uk
Website: www.bushwoodbooks.co.uk
Free postage in the U.K., Europe; air mail at cost.

Dedication

I like to dedicate my books to our children and grandchildren. Both of our sons were raised in Lancaster County. Dr. Alexander E. Richman, a mathematician, and his wife Elana, live across the river in neighboring York County. Our younger son, Dr. Joshua S. Richman, a medical researcher, and his wife Kristin are the parents of our grandchildren Benjamin David (7) and Zoë Elizabeth Anne (5). Alas, they live in Birmingham, Alabama—need I say more? They all reside outside of the true American Garden of Eden, Lancaster County.

17 CHHR 12

OUSE.
ONE PRICE HOUSE
NORTH QUEEN STREET, LANCASTER, PA.

61—State Hospital
for Crippled Children,
Elizabethtown, Pa.
2B342

Contents

Acknowledgments

Any project relies on the help and support of many people. Stephen Miller, the Director of the Landis Valley Museum, has been a major facilitator. I am also proud to claim him as a former graduate student. A professional leader and a humane administrator, he has helped to shape the modern Landis Valley Museum. My other colleagues at Landis Valley have also been helpful. Thank you, Marilyn Monath, Donna Horst, Bruce Bomberger, Tim Essig, Will Morrow, Joyce Perkinson, Cindy Reedy, Joe Schott, and Trish Frey. Of very special note is Michael Emery, Landis Valley Museum Educator and Volunteer Coordinator, who is a fount of knowledge about the Pennsylvania Germans and an avid collector of books, paper, and photographic memorabilia. He has shared many items with me and has ferreted out others. His fingerprints are clearly visible. Dr. Russell Eaton, a retired physicist who has undertaken the ongoing, almost Herculean, task of organizing the Landis Valley Museum's postcards, has also been very helpful. Craig Benner did all the original photography. As always, the Library staff at Penn State Harrisburg have performed their magic for me.

I am a technological idiot. Thankfully, kind people have taken pity. At the office Mike Emery always helps me with computer issues. I do not know, however, if I could function in this increasingly complex world without my wife, Dr. M. Susan Richman, mathematician and retired university dean. She is my major technology enabler and she has voluntarily transcribed the manuscript from my inelegant scrawl into useful and improved typescript. She, blessedly, is touched with the work ethic of her Pennsylvania German forbears.

I write about subjects I enjoy, focusing on Pennsylvania and New York topics. Over the years I have been inspired by many historians, especially Pennsylvanians.. The late S. K. Stevens, Donald H. Kent, Paul

A. Wallace influenced and mentored me when I was a young writer, as did the late John Aungst, past Director of the Lancaster County Historical Society. Special thanks go to three living scholars whose work continues to give me inspiration. First, Dr. John B. Frantz, a colleague from the Pennsylvania State University, Peter Seibert, a former student and now President of the Heritage Center of Lancaster County. In a class by himself is John Ward Willson Loose, who is simply "Mr. Lancaster History." The former longtime president of the Lancaster County Historical Society, he is a walking encyclopedia of Lancastriana and a living treasure. My last graduate student, Oscar Beisert, who completed his studies in 2007 at Penn State Harrisburg (where I taught for 38 years), provided an endless fountain of questions that helped keep me sharp. We have now adopted him into our family.

Preface

The most difficult task in creating this book was selecting the postcards, i.e., being limited in the number that could be illustrated. The variety of Lancaster County postcards is phenomenal. In the early 20th century every hamlet and crossroads boasted its postcard views. Specifically, Lancaster County is a center of agriculture and commerce, and the repository of a varied and significant heritage of national interest. It is also the nexus of a lively and economically important tourist industry. All have lent themselves to the creation of a treasure trove of postcards. While some cards included here are drawn from private collections, most are from the collections of the Landis Valley Museum in Manheim Township, Lancaster County, where the author is Director of Research and Development for the Heirloom Seed Project. This book is compiled for the benefit of the non-profit Landis Valley Associates, whose mission it is to help maintain and develop the Landis Valley Museum.

The Cottage
Bainbridge, Pennsylvania
2008

I. Lancaster and the Postcard

To be a Native Lancastrian

I love Lancaster County, but I know that I can never be considered a Lancastrian because I wasn't born here and, further, neither my parents nor my grandparents were either. This was driven home to me a few years ago when my wife and I went to welcome a new neighbor who had just moved in next door to our Lancaster County home, where we had lived for some thirty years. After the greeting the husband, hearing my New York-inflected speech said, "You're not from around here, are you?" They, of course, were natives. They moved to Bainbridge from the town of Maytown, 5 miles away! On a more public plane, *The Lancaster New Era,* Lancaster City's afternoon newspaper, which proudly claims to be the largest afternoon daily in Pennsylvania, in April, 2007, noted in a lead editorial:

> Periodically, newcomers with political ambitions move into Lancaster County and, after establishing themselves, happily tell us how they can provide leadership superior to what we now have.
>
> Inevitably, these highly confident, highly ambitious souls fail to see or appreciate subtle currents of thought and sentiment that swirl through the populace of this county.
>
> The outsiders get the basics. They understand that most people here are conservative in matters of finance, private and public. They know that county residents place high value on public safety and public order. They're aware countians expect leaders to have a record of solid, sustained achievements.
>
> But newcomers miss the nuances.
>
> They don't see that Lancaster countians also are liberal in their charitable giving, that they are resistant to government intrusion on personal privacy or property rights.
>
> And most often, they fail to understand that county residents expect leaders to temper their personal success with humility and with consistent contributions to community endeavors.

What constitutes an outsider in politics? – why, somebody who moved here "… two decades ago … [and the candidate and family] established a home and business here."

Together with the notion that a true Lancastrian is one born here, or at least of Lancastrian heritage, is the feeling of exceptionalism in which Lancastrians pride themselves. Gerry Lestz, who "… grew up on Shippen Street and never forgot that his grandparents fled persecution in Europe for being Jewish … "loves the county and at 92, the former newspaper man "… author, philanthropist and civic leader extraordinaire continues to write about and explore the history …" of his home county. "I think," Lestz rhapsodizes, "Lancaster is one of the most unusual communities in America. All you have to do is go 50 miles away to realize that's so." The nonagenarian gives many reasons for Lancaster's exceptionalism, centering on, "...its burgeoning art scene to its charitable generosity." Lestz looks to the future opining that "… the Lancaster community is on the threshold of its greatest expansion to date. And people who love Lancaster see how they can work to do even more." As a guardian of his region's past, Lestz purchased *Baer's Agricultural Almanac* in 1949, and he still oversees the running of what is one of America's oldest "Farmers Almanacs."

Concerts of the always improving Lancaster Symphony Orchestra proclaim the mantra, "Only in Lancaster" as the orchestra strives for unique programming.

Although Lancaster remains a basically conservative community with a strong Pennsylvania German heritage, there are many newcomers including a sizeable Hispanic community. Old timers grumble about traffic congestion in suburbanizing Lancaster County, but many are leaving the older town and city neighborhoods for suburbia at the same time that many younger people are moving back in to the more historic neighborhoods of Lancaster City. How much is the county changing? "The Rainbow Rose Community, a newly formed group for gay, lesbian, bisexual and transgender people, planned Lancaster's first gay pride event," reported the *New Era.* The event was scheduled for June 23, 2007 in Downtown Lancaster, but it never took place. Well, maybe change remains slow!

Lancaster in the Eighteenth Century

When William Penn established his colony of Pennsylvania in 1682, it had three counties – Philadelphia, Chester, and Bucks – and it was from Chester County that Lancaster County was "erected" or formed on May 10, 1729.

The early population included Quakers, Germans from Switzerland and the Palatinate, Scots Irish, and French Huguenots. These Huguenots, protestants who settled near modern Paradise and Strasburg, were led by a remarkable woman, Madame Marie Ferree. Most of the group would intermarry with the Germans and remnants of their names remain among the LeFevers, the Dillers, the Zellers, and others. There was also a smattering of Catholics and Jews. Lititz was established as a Moravian community in 1742 by followers of Count Nicholas von Zinzindorf and became a center of education and culture in the region. Lancaster County's unique religious community was the Ephrata Cloister, founded by the charismatic Conrad Beissel in the 1730s. Composed of cloistered and family divisions of Seventh Day Baptists, the society eventually withered away, but their communitarian buildings, medieval in style, survive as a museum administered by the Pennsylvania Historical and Museum Commission. The still highly visible sectarians, especially the Amish and the Mennonites, also arrived in the 18th Century.

Once the new Lancaster County was established, it was necessary to create a county seat where a courthouse and a gaol, or prison, would be built. The first Lancaster County Court was held at Postlethwaite's Tavern (near present Gap) in August, 1729; its first case was the trial of a thief, who was sentenced to a flogging. The most influential population, mainly Quakers, lived in a hamlet, Wright's Ferry (modern Columbia) on the Susquehanna River. They appeared to have the inside track to have their settlement named the county seat, but the demand went out for a more centrally located venue. This strong request, aided by the political acumen of landowner James Hamilton, led to the siting of Lancaster Townstead. Curiously, the community was established a mile from the Conestoga River, making it one of the first inland towns in America, one not built on a navigable waterway.

British Isles precedents were followed in plotting Lancaster. James Jones, a Philadelphia surveyor, along with James Hamilton himself, laid out the new town. The Courthouse would be located on Centre Square, the enlarged intersection of the two principle streets – one running north and south, the other east and west. Historian John Ward Willson Loose observed that street names could be used to demonstrate loyalty to the monarchy. Hence,

> The main east-west street, now High Street, would become King George Street, while the chief north-south road would honor his consort, Queen Caroline. Parallel to Queen Caroline Street would be Duke of Cumberland Street one block to the east, and Prince of Wales Street one block to the west. Orange Street would recognize the royal house of King William III. Identifications with English royalty were dropped from common usage long before the Revolution, those streets being called simply King, Queen, Duke, and Prince. Dear to the English heart was the custom for naming streets for trees, nuts, fruits, berries, and vines. James Hamilton was duty-bound to surround the royal streets with Chestnut, Lime, Lemon, Mulberry, and Vine streets. Water Street was a pathway along Roaring Brook ....

By 1740 Lancaster had about 140 developed lots and approximately 600 inhabitants. Fifteen years later "... British travelers remarked that Lancaster exceeded in size most inland towns in England" As the town grew markets were established and numerous craftsmen, including smiths and tanners, set up workshops. As a county seat and a small commercial center, Lancaster Townstead also needed taverns, which multiplied in number as the community grew. The best known of these was the White Swan built in 1754 and operated for many years by Matthias Slough, who would play a prominent role during the Revolution. It has been observed that every Lancaster County village, no matter how modest, had to contain a core of three businesses – a general store, a blacksmithy, and a tavern.

Lancaster's jail and workhouse complex was built about 1730, even before the courthouse, which wasn't erected until 1736-38. Both were fairly impressive brick buildings. The courthouse was destroyed by fire in 1784 and the jail was taken down in 1852 when the present Lancaster County Prison opened. Both buildings were the site of events of widespread significance. The most notorious of these was the Paxtang Massacre of December 27, 1763. A few days earlier, a band of 57 Scots-Irish Presbyterians from Paxtang (near present Harrisburg) had decided to do their part in helping eliminate the Indians who were giving settlers great problems on the frontier. Rather than taking their crusade west, the bunch came east and attacked a small community of peaceful Conestoga Indians living in present Manor Township. When the initial killing occurred most of the young able-bodied native Americans were out of their village, peddling baskets and other wares. Not deterred, the "Paxtang Boys" murdered the elderly and children they encountered. Lancaster County was outraged and alarmed and, to protect the survivors, authorities moved them to protective custody in the jail at Prince and King Streets. On the following Sunday morning, while the jailers and most other Lancastrians were at church, the Paxtang thugs broke into the jail and brutally massacred every man, woman, and child they found.

The courthouse was scene of events of State. Notorious Indian treaties were negotiated here in 1744 and it was also here, on September 27, 1777, that the Continental Congress, escaping from the British occupation of Philadelphia, met. In 1759 one John Jones was convicted of burglary, and "Negro York" was convicted of rape. Both were hanged, as was Catherine Fisher, the only woman ever executed in Lancaster County.

George Ross of Lancaster was a Signer of the Declaration of Independence and the document was first formally read on the courthouse steps on July 8, 1776. Some Lancastrians were loyalists but, perhaps, most were for the Revolution. Others were ambiguous. General "Mad" Anthony Wayne was frustrated by many of Lancaster's German population. Urging his Commissioner of Clothing to get garments for freezing soldiers, he exhorted him to find supplies, "... even if they had to take the pants off the Dutchmen." On a Sunday morning in 1777, a group of men famously met under an oak tree on the grounds of the Donegal Presbyterian Church to take an oath to the Revolutionary cause. The tree, which lasted until the late 20th century, was to become widely celebrated as the "Witness Tree." The church still thrives. Edward Hand came to America as a surgeon with an Irish regiment during the closing years of the French and Indian Wars. In 1774 he resigned his commission to practice medicine in Lancaster. With the coming of war, Hand became Adjutant General of the Revolutionary Army – and a close friend of Washington, who would visit him in Lancaster in 1791. Hand's home, Rock Ford, is now preserved as a museum.

When Congress met in Lancaster it arrived with a whole retinue, including British and Hessian prisoners of war. The common soldiers were contained in stockades while their officers were "paroled" into the community. One of these was young British Major John Andre, who lived in the home of Caleb Cope, a prominent plasterer and politician. After he left Lancaster, Andre became involved in Benedict Arnold's treason and was hanged for his deeds.

During the Revolution, Lancaster County was especially important because of its production of foods, cloth, leather and rifles. Lancaster was smack in the middle of "the breadbasket of America" and was a major producer of grain as well as pork and beef. Leathermaking was an important byproduct of meat packing. The Dutch famously used every part of the pig except the oink. The Pennsylvania Rifle (also known as the Kentucky Rifle) was invented in Lancaster County and many weapon makers were located in the Conestoga Valley. Most of the gun makers also made the more traditional, if less accurate, musket as well. Conflicts between the new government, local farmers, craftsmen and merchants were commonplace because Congress's agents were usually only empowered to pay for their goods with nearly worthless Continental paper currency. Wartime inflation boosted prices to levels that are high even to 21st century eyes. In 1780 in Lancaster eggs sold for $6 per dozen and butter for $12 per pound!

Many happenstances, as well as prices, normalized with the end of hostilities, and generally conservative Lancaster County became a stronghold for the Federalists, the party of Washington and Hamilton.

Lancaster, as an inland community, knew the importance of good roads; the Lancaster and Philadelphia Turnpike, begun in 1792, was the first major macadam-paved road in America. Regular stage routes made Lancaster City an attractive interim Capital City of Pennsylvania when the government left Philadelphia in 1799 and before it moved to the permanent Capital City, Harrisburg, thirteen years later.

Lancaster in the Nineteenth Century

As was to be expected, the borough's economy, which had boomed, then suffered after the state government left. Lancaster, as a consolation, was officially made a city in 1818, by act of the General Assembly.

As Lancaster successfully struggled to recover economically, America was grappling with unfinished business not settled in our Declaration of Independence and our Constitution. Principle among these was the issue of slavery and the still-existing debate over states' rights, which eventually led to the Civil War. Two Lancaster residents played pivotal national roles in events leading up to the War – and their influence helped shape Reconstruction: Thaddeus Stevens and James Buchanan, political enemies, who would both die in 1868.

Thaddeus Stevens (1793-1868) as a member of the Pennsylvania House of Representatives became known for advocating public education as "The Father of the Free School Act" in Pennsylvania. He was also active in radical politics, especially the Anti-Masonic Party. Settling in Lancaster and practicing law, he was an early advocate for the abolition of slavery. Club-footed from birth, he always sided with the underdog and attacked those he perceived to be aristocrats. Never married, his Lancaster properties were looked after by his housekeeper, Lydia Smith, a free woman of color. There were many rumors about the nature of their relationship. Property that Stevens and Smith owned is now being developed into a museum. Elected to Congress in 1859, Stevens was an advocate for war and afterwards he proudly became the "Father of the Reconstruction Acts," which sought to punish the South and give compensation to freed slaves. He was a leader in the movement to impeach and convict President Andrew Johnson, a native of Tennessee, and Lincoln's Vice President.

James Buchanan (1791-1868), "Old Buck" would be Pennsylvania's only native-born President. [Dwight David Eisenhower would famously retire to his Gettysburg, Pennsylvania, farm after his presidency.] Like Stevens, Buchanan was born outside of Lancaster, which was more acceptable when Lancaster was newer, and he too would become a lawyer and remain unmarried. But here similarities end. Buchanan was a mediator and conciliator where Stevens was a firebrand. Stevens was always a provincial while Buchanan was a cosmopolitan who served as American ambassador to the Court of Saint James. As the President (1857-1861) immediately preceding Lincoln, he is often excoriated today for being inept and responsible for the outbreak of the Civil War. Confrontation, however, was never his strong suit. Unfortunately for him, he was the "wrong man, in the wrong place, at the wrong time." His home, "Wheatland," is a prominent local museum.

The Civil War almost came into Lancaster County when Georgia troops under General John Brown Gordon started across the long Susquehanna river bridge into Columbia on June 28, 1863. After they were fought back, Lancastrians burned the bridge to protect the County from further sorties. Two Lancastrians attained special recognition in the war: Major General Samuel P. Heintzelman of Manheim and Lancaster City-born John Fulton Reynolds, who had turned down command of the Army of the Potomac and would die on the Gettysburg Battlefield. Lancaster's support of the War is memorialized in The Soldiers and Sailors Monument, which stands where the colonial-era courthouse had been built. Dedicated July 4, 1874, it presumably honors all veterans of wars but is it, in fact, the County's premier Civil War Monument.

Lancaster County's major rivers, the Susquehanna and the Conestoga, were never important navigational highways. Turnpikes helped with commerce but it was the coming of the railroad that would transform the county in many ways. Towns on the railroad line prospered, those bypassed languished. The railroads made dairying an important agricultural industry and led to the development of many of the county's other signature industries and commercial establishments, especially Hamilton Watch and The Armstrong Cork Works. Milton S. Hershey had his first success as a candy maker in Lancaster City. The money he made here manufacturing caramels would provide the capital to launch his chocolate empire. F. W. Woolworth opened his first store in Lancaster and built the company's first architectural showpiece here.

The Postcard's History

All of this history and many social changes took place within the photographic age, and especially in the age of the postcard, as is very effectively illustrated here through these media.

Photography was developed in France in the late 1830s and, by 1840, the first Daguerreotypists were at work in America. Where at one time having a likeness painted was available only to the privileged minority, now, through the miracle of photography, everyone could pose for a quick inexpensive portrait. As photography improved, many photographers turned their lenses on their surroundings and their towns. Visual information became widely available. How could it be shared? The picture postcard was an early answer.

First used in Europe, the American picture postcard was authorized by an Act of Congress on May 19, 1898, and new regulations were passed in 1901 that standardized size and, later, message space, and led to the American postcard boom, which was certainly at its heights before World War I. The fascination with postcards, which initially cost but a penny to mail, would remain strong until the 1970s and, to an extent, it still exists today. Every tourist site and museum offers postcards for visitors to buy as souvenirs and to send to friends and relatives, but the function is really different.

At the height of the postcard boom, these inexpensive images let people see what sites a few miles away looked like, as well as those across the world. It is interesting to see the number of surviving postcards mailed to people several miles distant, prior to 1905, when postcards could legally bear messages. Other cards simply showed off some local feature. Inexpensive photographic postcards allowed you to mail your own likeness to a friend. As the years went on postcards became our first commercial greeting cards and novelty and humorous cards evolved.

The Landis Valley Museum Postcard Collections

The postcard collections at Landis Valley Museum in Manheim Township, near Lancaster City, are very informative. Many were owned by the family who established the museum. While the founding brothers were George Diller Landis (1867-1954) and Henry Kinzer Landis (1865-1955), the bulk of the collection was acquired by their semi-invalid sister, Nettie May Landis (1879-1914) who apparently sent out hundreds or, perhaps, thousands of postcards, asking for cards in return. Thousands replied. The brothers bought postcards as well and Henry K., an amateur photographer had postcards printed from his own photographs. Along the way many contributions came from local families. The collection is a visual history of the world, especially dating from 1900 to 1925. The postcards became more episodic afterwards. The collection is eclectic, ranging from views of European castles, to early Christmas greetings, to an especially bizarre postcard showing slain Mexican hero/villain Pancho Villa. The many early Lancaster views are a testimony to civic pride and, seemingly, every structure of any pretense in the county is recorded.

Postcards in America

The early age of postcards coincides with the City Beautiful movement fostered by the White City at the World Columbian Exhibition in Chicago which had a riveting effect on America. It sparked an escalation of civic pride in thousands of communities, including those in Lancaster County. Coming at the same time as the rise of the postcard (Congress had even authorized special World's Fair postcards.) and the subsequent collecting frenzy, there was a great demand for cards that showed local vistas, public buildings and monuments, and the homes of the local elite. These were sent and collected by natives as well as tourists. From a historian's perspective, the most important of these views are of the same town or vista published ten or more years apart, which often show the dramatic changes a growing economy and a tourist industry wrought on the landscape.

The late 19th century also witnessed the emergence of vacations for the masses. Mostly, this phenomenon was expanded by the prosperity of the 1920s and the widespread availability of the automobile. After the 1930s and wartime, the booming postwar years fixed vacations into the American mainstream. This was also the era characterized as the golden age of illustration. The commercial imagery of J. C. Leyendecker (1874-1951), Howard Chandler Christy (1875-1952), James Montgomery Flagg (1877-1960), and others was adapted and reflected in the cards of the period.

As vacation travel developed, Lancaster County evolved a strong tourist industry based on the Pennsylvania German, and more specifically, the Amish culture. This is reflected on many thousands of cards. Adding to the mix are postcards promoting other tourist attractions that have grown up, piggybacking on the core enterprise.

Essentially, then, the Lancaster County postcards are bifurcated: those designed essentially for the hometown market and normative visitors, and those promoting the tourist trade. This, of course, reflects the reality of life in Lancaster County, just as life in contemporary Las Vegas, where you can live a life involved with what has become the outsider image of your community, casinos, or one that doesn't interact with these elements at all. Many contemporary Las Vegas residents never go to the fabled "Strip." Many contemporary Lancastrians never go near a farm or a tourist concentration – if they can help it.

Postcards are life mirrors held up to a society. Most provide you with a straightforward image; some, however, like funhouse looking glasses, deliver some bizarre distortions!

II. The Red Rose City

Two feuding English royal lines, the Lancastrians and the Yorks, adopted the rose as their symbol. York's was white and Lancaster's red. In the late 19th century and into the post-World War II era, beds of the flowers greeted visitors to the communities named after these royal houses. When the cities' minor league baseball teams play today, local media call their contests "The War of the Roses." The rose and lilac card was printed in Germany. "Greetings from Lancaster, Pa.," --in glitter-- was probably added locally. The composite card dates from c.1950 and was published in Chicago by Curt Teich and Company. L, N, A, T, and R feature Amish vignettes. A, C, S, and E are Lancaster City landmarks.

Centre Square was the hub of a very busy Lancaster early in the 20th century. Standing on the site of the colonial courthouse is the Soldiers and Sailors Monument, which was dedicated July 4, 1876. The figure, the "Genius of Liberty," surmounts it and faces north. The new Watt and Shand Department Store dominates a principal corner. Strongly influenced by the Chicago architectural style of the firm of Adler and Sullivan, its façade is being preserved while a modern hotel and convention center are being built behind it. The landmark was designed by Lancaster architect Cassius Emlen Urban (1863-1939), who also did the now-demolished dual-towered Woolworth building.

City Hall was built (1795-1798) to serve as public offices to serve the nearby second Lancaster County Courthouse, which stood where the Soldier and Sailors' Monument now stands. When the present Courthouse was constructed, the old one was sold to the City of Lancaster, which used it until 1932. Today it houses the Heritage Center of Lancaster County, as does the adjoining (to the left) Masonic Lodge Hall and market spaces, built 1798-1799. To the right of the Heritage Center is the grand Romanesque Revival Central Market, designed by architect James H. Warner and finished in 1889. Printed in Germany, the card was mailed in 1907 to a woman in Elizabethtown.

King Street is Lancaster City's principle east-west street and, where it crosses the square, it was the hub of urban life. The views date from c. 1905-1915. The romantic night view was, no doubt, taken during the day and then altered by an artist to appear to have been done after dark. It was mailed in 1914 to Miss Annie Bender, in Port Royal, Pennsylvania. "Dear Friend Annie," it reads, "I like it down here see lots of nice things and ride in the street cars and go to the Moving pictures am going to Pequea on Independence Day." It is signed, "Lovingly Anna."

North Queen Street was an important commercial hub early in the 20th century. Before the automobile, travel was by horse drawn vehicles or trolley car. "One Price House" was a store mimicking the success of F. W. Woolworth's "5 & 10 Cent" stores, where everything sold for a nickel or a dime. A sign on the building on the extreme right advertises a dentist. Dominating the streetscape is the Woolworth Building of 1898, designed by Lancaster County-born Cassius Emlen Urban.

The Chicago-style Conestoga Building represented the latest in commercial architecture and housed the offices of one of the era's high-tech firms –"Electric Light and Power." Mailed in 1914, from Lancaster to Leacock, the message on the reverse invites a country resident to visit the big city.

Curb markets were an ancient institution in downtown Lancaster until outlawed in 1927. Among the most popular sites were those held on and near the courthouse steps on East King Street. Markets today continue to be held in Central Market, built in 1889, as seen in this 1960s card.

Downtown boasted many department stores, now all gone. The most architecturally distinctive were the buildings of Watt and Shand (see above) and "The New Hagar Store." Both, adaptively reused, remain highly visible Lancaster landmarks. J. Miehle & Sons proudly promoted the size of their store with a 1907 postcard noting the South Aisle [is] "230 feet deep." Leinbach's Daylight Department Store featured skylights and lots of vegetation. Rehabbed, it is now offices.

Lasting as a family-owned enterprise into the 21st century, Demuth's Tobacco Shop, under new ownership, is still in business. It is one of the oldest firms in Pennsylvania. The trademark tobacco store figure is believed to have been carved by a family member, Johannes Demuth (c.1750-1820). The buildings of the Demuth complex are owned by the Demuth Foundation, which preserves the memory of the important Lancaster born American artist, Charles Demuth (1883-1935).

Wheatland Hotel, Lancaster, Pa.

HOTEL BRUNSWICK, LANCASTER, PA.

Hotels became central to the life of Lancaster City. Its premier hostelry was the grand Hotel Brunswick, celebrated for its Baron Stiegel Room restaurant, and designed by Cassius Emlen Urban in 1914 and 1922. Torn down in 1965, it was replaced with a far inferior hotel that is still struggling to find an identity. A 1930s card is testimony to the original hotel's status. A handwritten note on the back reads, "May 6th 1936 Ben Maurice Omar and I had lunch here in connection with the Nineteenth Annual Meeting of the Hougenots [sic] Society of Pennsylvania." The only still-standing hotel building in Lancaster is the Wheatland on Orange Street, which no longer serves its original purpose.

The Stevens House was named for the famed Lancaster citizen, Thaddeus Stevens, who was recently deceased when the hotel opened in 1874. The c.1910 view shows the hotel as enlarged by Cassius Emlen Urban. It was a favorite of visiting theatre people who performed in the nearby Fulton Opera House and Lancaster's other theatres. The view was published by "I. Steinfeldt, Lancaster, Pa." The legend on the reverse of the "Historic English Dining Room," informs us that it "... has not only excellent food but also many interesting pictures and mementos on the walls. Recommended by Duncan Hines for both rooms and food, "the Stevens House in Lancaster, Pennsylvania is centrally located and on Routes 30, 72, 222 and 230." Along with Lancaster movie theatres, the hotel was a victim of urban renewal in the 1960s.

STEVEN'S HOUSE, LANCASTER, PA.

Historic English Dining Room
Stevens House, Lancaster, Pa.

"The Village" in downtown Lancaster was a tourist attraction that included "America's Most Unique Bus Depot." The "C.T. Art Colortone" card was printed by Curt Teich & Co. of Chicago circa 1950.

The YMCA and the YWCA both appealed (and still appeal) to conservative Lancaster, dedicated as they are to helping foster moral behavior among the young. Established locally in the 1870s, the YMCA building seen in this late 1920s card is no longer. The YWCA's handsome Georgian Revival building still stands at North Duke and East Orange. The card was published by "Morrison Bros. News Agency, Lancaster, Pa."

The Hamilton Club has long been Lancaster's premier social club. Founded in 1889, it has been housed for many years in the Chateau-esque mansion built for Catherine Haldeman Long in the 1890s. This card circa 1915 was mailed by Ida M. Diller of 137 S. Prince Street to a friend in Halifax, Nova Scotia.

Lancaster Free Public Library proudly traces its origins to the private subscription, Lancaster Library Company of 1759. The view is mid-20th century and was distributed by "I. Steinfelt, Lancaster, Pa."

The Lutheran Church of the Holy Trinity is Lancaster City's most impressive colonial era structure. The church's first recorded service was held in 1729 and the current edifice was begun in 1761. When the steeple was completed in 1794, Lancaster had the tallest building in Pennsylvania, west of Philadelphia. Strongly influenced by the London church designs of Sir Christopher Wren, the steeple is ornamented by statues of the four evangelists believed to have been carved by Johannes Demuth (c.1750-1820). Today the wooden originals are housed in the church; metal replicas stand on the tower. In the 1950s, Victorian buildings were demolished and a Colonial Revival Parish House was constructed in 1953-1954 for this still vital congregation. The card was mailed in 1905 to Miss May Diller of Lancaster by her friend Florence in Gap.

Gothic Revival was popular in building many of Lancaster's 19th century churches. The card of resolutely English Gothic St. John's Episcopal Church was mailed to Milton F. Gety of Ephrata in 1912. The one of the more stately cut stone St. Paul's Reformed Church, mailed in February 1908, bears a playful message. On the front "Miss Emelia Link" informs that, "I have not been waiting at the church." This on a card sent to 'Mr. H. Palmer of 35 Mulberry ST." Was romance, or merely flirtation, in the air?

Lancaster has had a Jewish presence since the 18th century; however, its oldest Jewish congregation is Temple Shaarai Shomayim, founded in 1855. During the 1880s the congregation, begun as an orthodox group, affiliated with the Reform Movement. In 1895, it constructed a new synagogue at Duke and James street combining elements of the Neo-Classical and Moorish Revival styles. It is among the oldest synagogue buildings in continuous use in America. The congregation's earlier home at Orange and Christian Streets now houses the Lancaster County Bar Association.

The Fulton Opera House as it appeared c.1910. Built by Christopher Hager in 1852 as Fulton Hall, it was a large level-floored meeting hall with a stage along one wall. The ornate theatre interior was installed in 1873. For years it was a venue for vaudeville, plays, and occasional opera, as well as a movie theatre. It is the only historic theatre remaining in Lancaster City. Now owned and operated by a cultural not-for-profit organization, it has been extensively restored and modernized. A statue of Robert Fulton ornaments the Italianate façade.

The old Pennsylvania Railroad Station at North Queen and East Chestnut Streets brought the trains right downtown. Mailed in 1911, from a son to his father, it bears a comic legend. Now a parking lot, the building was abandoned when the new Pennsylvania Railroad Station was completed in 1928.

The Georgian Revival front pavilion of the Elks home was new when this card was mailed in 1920.

Lancaster's ornate Moorish and Renaissance Revival City Hall was originally built as the Post Office. The card, mailed in 1910, has an enigmatic message on the front.

The third Lancaster County Courthouse, built according to designs drawn by Samuel Sloan (1815-1884), an important Philadelphia architect, is seen in two views: one c. 1905 and the other one in 1970. As you look west on East King Street, you see the newly remodeled Garvin's Department Store and Lancaster's sole "skyscraper," the Greist Building named for Republican Congressman William W. Greist (1858-1929) and designed in 1923 by Cassius Emlen Urban. The view from the top of the Greist building was mailed in 1932.

North Duke Street, early in the 20th century, was an elite residential address. The trolley car made it simple to get around town.

Lancaster Theological Seminary was originally the Reformed Theological Seminary when founded in 1825 in Carlisle. Its grand Romanesque Revival dark brick building was designed by Cassius Emlen Urban. Built adjacent to the now secular Franklin and Marshall College (the spires of its Old Main are visible above the trees), it has trained generations of clergy.

Franklin and Marshall College was formed by the merger of Lancaster's Franklin College and Mercersburg's Marshall College in 1853. Old Main, a Collegiate Gothic structure was built in 1856. The school's library is later. Mailed In September of 1910 to Paul Rabenold of Reading, it was probably sent by a proud freshman to a friend. "Hello there old scout. How's the cutting. F & M is a fine place. Got Harvard beat all to a frazzle."

Franklin and Marshall Academy, a private boys prep school housed in a handsome, now destroyed, Georgian Revival building, was closed in 1942 during World War II. The postcard, published by Morrison Brothers News Agency of Lancaster, was mailed In 1938.

Twentieth century high schools. Renaissance style Stevens High School for Girls was built in 1904; and a Boys High School followed in 1916. Both became elementary schools in 1938 upon the completion of Moderne coeducational McCaskey High School, designed by Henry Y. Shaub. Stevens High is an especially fine building with a marvelous third floor auditorium. In the late 20th century it was converted into high-end apartments. Expanded and remodeled, McCaskey, named for a politically important former Lancaster Mayor, John Piersal McCaskey, whose term was 1906-1910, remains Lancaster's high school. When built at a cost of $900,000, McCaskey was the largest high school in Pennsylvania.

The Lancaster County Alms House and Asylum buildings were constructed in the 1870s-1890s. Now demolished, the structures are the site of Conestoga View, a once county-owned and operated nursing home. This uniquely annotated card was sent by a new staff member, probably a physician, to a friend in New York City in 1907.

Lancaster General Hospital was already an impressive building in 1907 when this card was mailed. St. Joseph's Hospital, built in the late 19th century, reflects the active Roman Catholic presence in Lancaster, which traces its history to the 18th century. In the 1950s the antiquated complex was torn down and replaced with a modern, expanded complex. Reflecting 21st century trends, Lancaster General Hospital has grown to a giant institution with two campuses; St. Joseph's has been sold to a national corporation and is operated as Lancaster Regional Medical Center.

The H. G. Long Home was established in honor of Henry G. Long, whose portrait appears over the fireplace in the Memorial Room. It remains housed in the enlarged mansion built by his widow, Catherine, whose town house became the Hamilton Club. It is now an assisted living facility.

The Children's Home was built in the 1860s as an orphanage. Obsolete because of societal changes, it was demolished in the 1950s. The site at the corner of East End Avenue and Ann Streets is now occupied by the Garden Court Apartments.

Set amidst lush landscape, the Lancaster County Prison, designed by Philadelphia architect Samuel Sloan (1815-1884) was built in 1851 for $110,000. Castlated, the Gothic Revival prison was influenced by John Haviland's earlier, and famed, Eastern State Penitentiary in Philadelphia. Our castle was constructed of a red (or Cocalico) sandstone, which was quarried at Konigmacher Quarry near Ephrata. An aerial view of the prison, c. 1930, even shows a formal garden inside its walls. Extensively remodeled and expanded after 1972, the structure has lost most of its picturesque quality.

A house at 533 South Prince Street has a unique history in that it was built in 10 hours in 1873. After winning an earlier bet that he could build a house in 24 hours, bitters manufacturer and self-promoter extraordinary, Benjamin Mishler, took the ten-hour bet – and won. The Lancaster County Historical Society has a photographic record documenting its construction.

By early in the 20th century, a city of any pretension needed a country club, where golf and tennis could be played among a select "smart set." This card mailed early in the century to "Mr. Horace C. Palmer, Tennessee Ave., Alt. [sic] NJ" has a very interesting message about the "good old summertime". "Horace please remember the Fralingers Salt Water Taffy, and send me a postcard to Mt. Gretna, Pa Camp-meeting Grounds. Well stay a week. ... Gus"

Barrose Terrace along the Conestoga Creek (now River) looks like a lost garden treasure of Lancaster. In fact, it was a combination show garden and nursery that specialized in roses. The owner family's name was Barr. The postal cards date from the 1930s.

The standpipe, or water tower, in Reservoir Park was designed to look like a romantic European tower. Water from the Conestoga was pumped to the large reservoir at the tower's base, near East King Street. Fittingly, there were several fountains installed in the park. The most sensational of these is the Lion Fountain carved by Blanche Nevin (c. 1838-1925), one of America's pioneer woman sculptors. Both cards were mailed c.1910.

Long Park was strongly influenced by the Olmstead tradition of creating beautiful landscapes for the enjoyment of city-dwellers, most famously seen in New York City's Central Park.. The card was mailed by a Lancaster resident to a friend who has taken a new job in that city. Printed on the obverse is, "VIEW IN LONG PARK. This visitor walks beside the beautiful artificial lake, a specimen of the carefully selected and highly cultivated floral preserves, and a promenade bordered with trees that, comparatively still in infancy, give promise of much added beauty in their maturity...."

Rocky Springs Park, along the Conestoga just east of the city, was one of many "trolley parks" developed in America in the late 19th century, most of whose patrons arrived by the new public conveyance. The park was once home to one of the largest east coast roller coasters and an enormous merry-go-round manufactured by the Denzel Company of Brooklyn, N.Y. Here, too, you could board a steamboat, one of a fleet of three, to cruise the Conestoga. After a long decline, the park finally closed in 1980.

Maple Grove Park was a popular amusement park that evolved from West End Park, a trolley-era picnic grove operated by Aaron Summy , who is credited with planting the many maple trees that would give the place its name. From 1912 into the 1950s Maple Grove Park was operated as an amusement park. The pool, once one of Pennsylvania's largest, lasted into the late 20th century when it failed structurally. It had held 1,500,000 gallons of water. The only remnant of the former parkland is the burned-out ruin of the Abbeville Mill, an important park landmark that stands along Columbia Avenue.

Park-like urban cemeteries, entered through impressive gates, became popular in American in the late 19th century. Lancaster has its share of these impressive necropolises, as witnessed by these cards, c. 1905. Cemeteries were popular tourist sites as well as substitutes for parks.

The graves of three of Lancaster's prominent 19th century citizens are marked by impressive monuments. General Reynolds and President Buchanan were buried in fashionable park like cemeteries. Stevens had insisted on being buried in an urban cemetery in which African Americans could also be interred.

After World War II cemeteries, like population centers, went suburban and, following the lead of Forest Lawn Cemetery in Los Angeles, offered visual attractions to increase visitation and help sell grave sites. The legend on the reverse of this 1980s card informs readers: "Planted in mid-May this World's Largest Floral Clock, 32 feet in diameter and containing 6000 living colored plants keeps good time and is enjoyed by thousands of annual visitors to Conestoga Memorial Park Cemetery, Lancaster Pa. Visitors also enjoy the cascade water falls and the twin lakes which abound with wildfowl."

III. The Rural Dream

Rural Lancaster County is beautiful settled landscape. This was especially true in the early 20th Century before suburban development. The view looking west from Rocky Springs emphasizes the rolling, well watered terrain. The intimate view along the Cocalico Creek, near Ephrata, is evocative of the best of rural America.

One of the most common images found on early cards is a horse-drawn vehicle, on a dirt road, traveling along a flower-bordered lakeside. These were often stock photographs that bore numerous legends. This one mailed in 1924 delivers greetings from "Strasburg, Pa."

Streams and the Susquehanna River appear on many postcards. The river had many swimming places. "Ship Rock: in Pequea Creek was a local landmark. While our waterways are usually peaceful, flooding and flash flooding can cause dramatic effects. The card with the debris strewn creek bank was taken near Lititz and mailed on a March 20 early in the last century. Hannah H. Wissler of "R. No. Lititz, Pa" writes simply to Calvin H. Miller of Ephrata. "On the other side you can see the results of Monday afternoon."

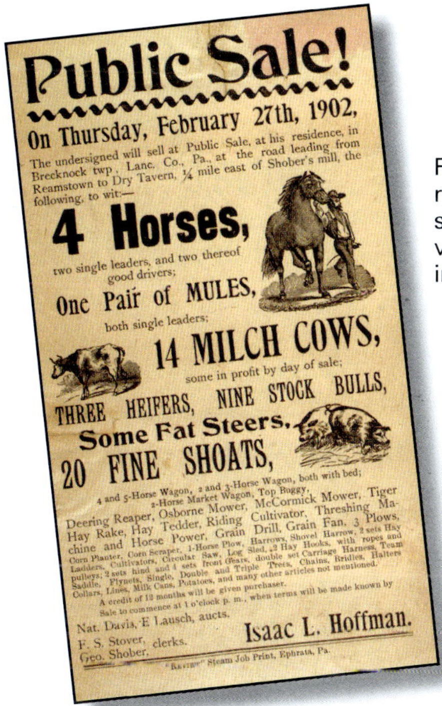

Farming is the hallmark of rural Lancaster County. Farm sale leaflets and posters are very valuable as windows into past farming practices.

Two bonnet-clad girls, distracted by visiting chickens, pause from their chores in the barnyard of a German farm. They are probably cleaning flax during the linen making process.

A group gathers in the front yard of Postlethwait's Tavern, which was the site of the first court sessions held in Lancaster County. Much remodeled, the house has lost its center chimney. A typical picket fence faces the road. Notice that the barn and house are on axis, as was usual on Pennsylvania Dutch farms.

Robert Fulton (1765-1807), a talented painter and the inventor of the steamboat, was born on a farm in rural Lancaster County.

A stock farm is one that specializes in raising cattle and/or horses. The Clare Point Stock Farm near Ephrata was a prosperous enterprise with many buildings. Note the center chimney stone house to the left and the house and barn on axis in the background.

After being cut, grain (probably wheat, as shown here) was tied into bundles and stacked before being taken to the barn area.

On small farms, the whole family often pitched in at grain harvest time. On larger places, the harvest was mainly brought in by men, especially hired workers, with the women cooking for the hungry crew.

Hand harvested corn was often husked in the field. These men proudly show the results of their work.

Steam tractors and other engine-driven machines changed grain culture. Bagged grain and straw bales are in the middle-right in this thrashing re-enact ment using machinery.

Open slats on a barn declare that it is for tobacco and filled with freshly harvested plants that need to air dry or cure.. A pumpkin field spreads through the foreground, ready for harvest.

A 2707 A Rural Scene near Ephrata, Pa.

Dairy cows in bucolic surroundings were a favorite subject for 19th century landscape painters as well as later postcard publishers. The hand-colored card is a stock view, probably sold in many areas. The scene near Ephrata is highly specific as a carriage pauses crossing a bridge over the stream. The "Famous Stockyard Inn," which has been in business for over a century, still operates at the edge of what was once the largest stockyard east of Chicago. The Inn featured Black Angus steaks on their menu. These Angus beefs pose in a Lancaster County cornfield on an advertising card, circa 1960, manufactured in Boston from a photograph done by a Mt. Joy, Pa., photographer.

In the years following the Civil War, tobacco was king in Lancaster County. Extremely profitable, although labor-intensive to produce, farmers called it, "The Mortgage Burner." It lost its luster as a crop only with the rise of the antismoking sentiment of the late 20th century. On larger farms various members of a family often had their own tobacco patches. One of these patches was even cultivated by 92-year-old Eliza Gochnauer! After the mature plants were cut, they were speared onto laths and hung on scaffolds to be loaded onto special wagons used to transport the harvested plants to the tobacco barns for drying and storage. Lancaster City became the center of a lively and economically important trade in tobacco.

OLD CONESTOGA WAGON OF LANCASTER, PA.

The Conestoga Wagon, drawn by four or six horses, was important for getting agricultural goods to market. The very heavy wagon's bowed bottom prevented loads from shifting. Developed in Lancaster County in the 18th century, their use continued into the age of railroad. Traditionally, the wagon master rode on the back left horse. In one view a helper stands on the retractable "lazy board." The assistant might sit on the board to rest from the more usual pastime of walking alongside the wagon. A range of 18th and 19th century Conestoga Wagons are in the collection of the Landis Valley Museum.

Covered bridges provided relatively inexpensive spans to cross a river, a creek, or a stream. The superstructure protected the roadbed from the weather. The Old Factory Bridge: is long gone but the 98-foot-long Bowers Bridge, built in 1888 and surrounded by Amish farmland, remains useful to local residents and is popular with tourists.

Donegal Presbyterian Church was built by Scots-Irish farmers and merchants. Shown in an early 20th century view, the inside walls were plastered but unpainted. The congregation worshiped in an unheated interior until the church was remodeled in 1851. Since being restored, it remains the center of an active congregation. During the Revolution men gathered under an oak tree outside the church to pledge their allegiance to the new political order. The "Witness Tree" survived well into the 20th century.

Stone arch bridges were favored, although expensive, spans and some built for turnpike use could even support the weight of railroads, as seen in the Mt. Joy example. The surfaces of most bridges, however, were earth covered, matching common road surfaces. Built by Abraham Witmer in 1800 (not the 1798 stated on the card), the nine-arched Witmer Bridge spanned the Conestoga. Too narrow to carry motor traffic on Lincoln High East, it was demolished in 1930. Another image of the bridge is shown in Chapter IV.

The Yeates School shown in this c. 1910 card was one of a number of small private schools, or academies that dotted the county. It was named for lawyer and delegate to the Constitutional Convention, Jasper Yeates (1745-1817), who had a country house near Gap.

Disasters sometimes struck Lancaster County. A breaking ice dam crushed these buildings along a county waterway, c. 1900, as seen in a photograph from G. H. Werntz of 23E Orange Street, Lancaster.

Freak winds and tornados have occasionally wreaked havoc on Central Pennsylvania farms, as witnessed in this destruction, c. 1910. The house shorn of its facade probably once had two front doors. The inverted barn once stood on axis with the house.

Nothing changed the face of rural Lancaster County as much as the automobile, which became a popular image on postcards. The humorous card was mailed in 1913. The unhappy storm-battered car was photographed c. 1910.

IV. Industry; The Machine in the Garden

Photo by [illegible] 1908 STONEROAD'S MILL, BUILT 1770, SOUTH-WEST OF LANCASTER, PA.

Grain mills were vital to an agricultural area. Built in the 18th and early 19th centuries, many were obsolete by the early 20th century when these cards were printed (circa. 1905-1915), but they were appreciated as picturesque historic landmarks. The oldest mill pictured, Stoneroad's Mill, nestled against a covered bridge, was constructed in 1770. Almost as old, but apparently derelict, was Eshelman's Mill, which also served as a gun barrel factory during the War of 1812. Garber's Mill was, apparently, converted to steam power (note the chimney) and was probably still in use when this photograph was taken in 1911. Rank's, or City Mill, a mid-19th century brick building, stood next to an extensive dammed millpond. *(Continued on following page)*

Photo D.B.L. 1910 ESHELMAN'S MILL (GUN BARREL FACTORY 1812) MILL CREEK CO., PA.

Fortunately for the aroma of our air, we no longer manufacture paper in Lancaster County, as we did in Eden when this photo was taken by D. B. Landis in 1911. Landis was "Publisher, Pluck Art Printer, Lancaster, Pa.," which produced this card. Another paper mill, accompanied by a box factory, was located in Lititz.

Lancaster County in the early 20th century was the center of the silk manufacturing industry in America. Cocoons imported from the far east were processed into thread and woven into cloth in several mills spread around the county. One in Lancaster City, the Rossmere mill owned by the Stehli Silk Corporation, was touted as the "Largest Silk Mill in the World." At its height it employed over 2000 workers. This card was sent early in the 20th century to Miss Reba M. White of Farmington, New Hampshire, by Nettie May Landis of "Landis Valley, Pa.," sister of the founders of the Landis Valley Museum.

The iron industry has been important in Lancaster County since pre-Revolutionary War days. Iron forges converted cast iron into the more malleable wrought iron needed by blacksmiths. The "Lower Forges," located in Colemanville in Conestoga Township, was owned by the ubiquitous Coleman Family, whose iron holdings were extensive in Central Pennsylvania. Nearby Martic Forge gave its name to a location still found on the map.

Follmer, Clogg and Company made Lancaster, "the umbrella capital of the world." It specialized in manufacturing "bumbershoots," large, family-sized black silk umbrellas, as well as beautiful feminine delights. Located at West King and Mulberry Streets, the building has been converted into apartments.

In addition to iron, various metals, including lead, nickel, and zinc, were mined and processed in Lancaster County. The dismantled zinc furnaces were photographed in 1910 near Bamfordville in East Hempfield Township. They were probably originally created by metals entrepreneur Charles Bamford.

The long-lived Brunnerville Iron Foundry was founded in 1850 in Warwick Township, 2 miles north of Lititz. The reverse of this c. 1960 card reads: "Inside [the] 100 year old "pouring room," workmen are molding "peepee: troughs, iron kettles, bull frog door stops, skillets and cricket boot jacks. Double-action 1850 crane used during "molding and breaking-out" period pivots on hand-cut stone base."

Hamilton Watch Company became famous for its "watch of railroad accuracy." The watch industry began in Lancaster in 1894 with a firm called "Adams and Perry." After a series of bankruptcies, the Hamilton Watch Company emerged in 1892. At its height the plant covered two entire blocks fronted on Columbia Avenue. Hamilton Park, south of the plant, became home to many of the factory's employees. Hamilton's landmark building is seen on a postcard mailed in 1906. This section of the factory has been converted into the Clock Tower Apartments.

Armstrong Cork Company and Lancaster have become synonymous, but the company was actually founded in Pittsburgh. Its Lancaster presence can be traced to 1895, when it acquired the Lancaster Cork Works. In 1905-1907 the Armstrong Cork Company built a huge linoleum plant in Lancaster and in 1929 it moved its corporate headquarters here. Encouraging its employees to be involved in the community, many of them became civic leaders. In recent years, the company has been downsizing its presence in Lancaster County. After going into bankruptcy as a result of its use of asbestos, a new Armstrong Corporation emerged from bankruptcy in 2007. The earlier card is c. 1910. The later one was mailed in 1943.

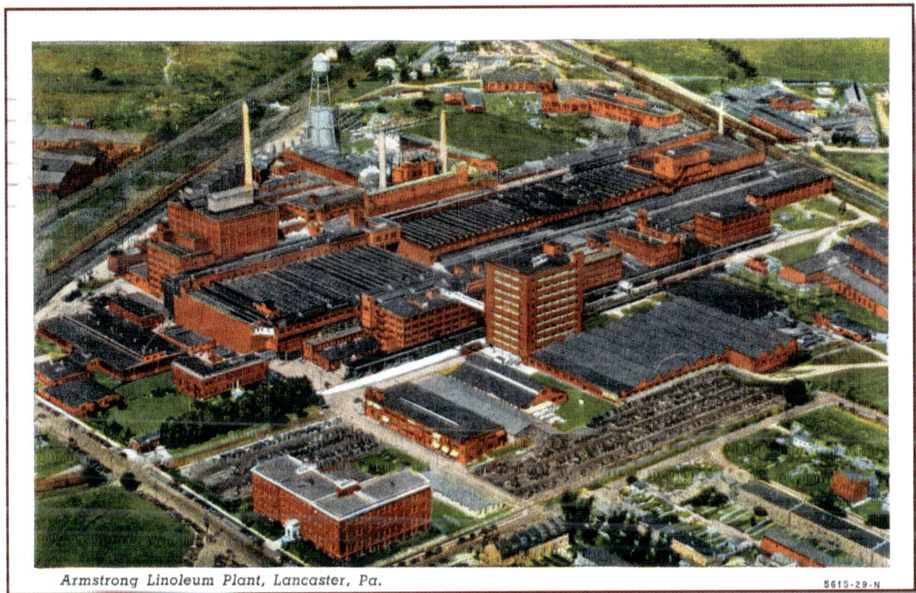

Since the 18th century, Lancaster has been a cattle trading center. When this postcard was printed c. 1910, the Union Stockyards, originally owned by the Pennsylvania Railroad, were handling about 60,000 head of cattle a year and it was said to be the largest stockyard east of Chicago. Operating into the end of the 20th century, the site's ultimate re-use is in question.

Witmer's Bridge, built in 1800, was an important link between Lancaster City and the countryside. Before the railroads stock was often driven over this route. The bridge was a great improvement over "Deering's Ford," where animals and humans had to cross previously. The bridge's history and fate is described in Chapter III. This 1905 card was printed in Germany and distributed by the Rotograph Company of New York City.

The stone arch Pennsylvania Railroad bridge, built in 1888, frames the city's contemporary steam-powered water pumping station along the Conestoga River. The bridge replaced an earlier wrought iron truss bridge. It stood at the site of the present West Walnut Street extension. The pumping station delivered water to a reservoir between King and Orange Streets. The plant was demolished in 1976, being replaced by a smaller, more modern, facility on the Susquehanna River near Columbia. Night scenes had a certain romance; however, they were usually photographed in daylight and artist-enhanced to give the nighttime illusion.

The Pennsylvania Railroad's trestle bridge over the Pequea Creek near Martic Forge was locally celebrated for its grace and as an engineering marvel. The black and white card was mailed in 1907 to Miss Gussie Palmer of 35 N. Mulberry Street, Lancaster. It is postmarked "Shoff," which is a small community almost in the bridge's shadow.

The Columbia and Wrightsville Ferry, shown on a card mailed in 1908, moved people between Lancaster and York Counties in the 19th and early 20th centuries. Behind it is the 6000-foot long steel Pennsylvania Railroad bridge across the Susquehanna.

A local ferry crosses the Susquehanna from Marietta, heading to a York County destination. The Ferry dock is visible on the riverbank beyond the line of rowboats, probably used by fishermen. The card was mailed to a Lancaster woman in 1906.

The Susquehanna Canal parallels the Pennsylvania Railroad at the base of Chickies Rock near Columbia, as pictured on a card mailed in 1908. Also note the new utility poles, not yet wired. Chickies Rock is a county landmark. Near its summit was an amusement park, accessible by a trolley line from Columbia. Looking south from its high elevations you still see stunning views of the Susquehanna. Looking north into the Donegal Valley you could clearly see the canal, the railroad, and the, now vanished, iron works of this once industrialized site.

Klein's Chocolate Company in Elizabethtown was founded by a contemporary of Milton S. Hershey of nearby Derry Township, Dauphin County. In the late 20th century the still active firm, represented by this pre-World War II postcard, was sold to M. and M. Mars, which makes many of its signature candies here. In 2007 the factory is being greatly expanded in size. The former Klein home outside of town is now used by a charitable foundation.

SAFE HARBOR WATER POWER CORP. POWER PLANT AND DAM, NEAR LANCASTER, PA. 3A233

Safe Harbor Dam and its power plant were constructed in the 1930s to help stimulate the Depression Era economy. Located in a, once remote, area of southern Lancaster County, a village was built to house construction and maintenance workers. The private utility that now owns the facility also owns thousands of acres of land on both sides of the river, of which it is ready to divest. Most is in the process of becoming parkland.

Lancaster County entered the nuclear age without an atomic powered electric plant on its soil, but with two that abut it. The oldest, shown in this card mailed in 1964, is the Peach Bottom Atomic Power Station in York County across the Susquehanna River from southwestern Lancaster County. Up river, just north of the Dauphin County line, is the Three Mile Island plant site of the infamous 1979 accident. Atomic energy plants require great amounts of water – which the Susquehanna can provide. In central Pennsylvania it is a river richly populated by hydro, coal-fired and nuclear power plants.

V. Small Towns; Main Street and Beyond

Even tiny Bainbridge on the Susquehanna bragged about its activity level. Mailed in the winter of 1913 to Miss Lula Brooks in Linden, Pennsylvania, Jim writes, "I am coming home Wed or Thursday to stay.... I almost froze coming to Bainbridge another fellow and I drove. I will see you Sat eve if you will be home. ..."

Some small towns even had home-decorated cards done on printed blanks. "I AM tickled with Conestoga Pa." features a real feather, a splint, and a ribbon.

Bridges across the Susquehanna are part of the lore of Columbia. It was here that a bridge was burned during the Civil War to keep back Southern invaders. A railroad bridge is seen beyond the "WRIGHTSVILLE-COLUMBIA BRIDGE. ... constructed in 1930 at a cost of $3,000,000." Locals on boats are still a familiar sight on the river.

Columbia, an important town since the 18th century, is sited on the Susquehanna and is lyrically seen in a circa 1905 card. Trolley lines connected Columbia with Lancaster City, and even went into the heights overlooking the town, including Laurel Hill and Chickies Hill, which sported a small amusement park, Chickies Park.

Up until the post-World War II days, the business district in the center of Columbia was very vibrant. Most of the buildings on the left hand side of this circa 1910 card are still there. The awnings and the streetcar are gone.

Founded by English Quakers in the 18th century, by the late 19th century, Columbia had a substantial Roman Catholic population, which constructed impressive institutional buildings, including St. Peter's Church and Convent and the very European-looking chapel in the St. Joseph Convent.

Lititz, in black and white (c. 1905) and color (c. 1960). Horse drawn vehicles and trolley cars shared the town's unpaved streets. Today the car rules, as in this view along Main Street.

Historic Manheim, named for Mannheim in Germany, is famed, in part, for its association with "Baron" Stiegel (1729-after 1797) and its large Market Square. The legend "Heart of Manheim Pa." is made of thick felt and stapled to the card, which was printed in 1907. The view of the unpaved Square was mailed in 1913. The black-and-white view is circa 1950.

Early in the 20th century almost every town had its trolley station, like that in tiny Martic Forge. Never mailed, the card bears a message written in 1907, describing a trip to the big city of Lancaster.

New Holland had trolley car tracks along its unpaved principal thoroughfare when "MAIN STREET,--West from Custer Ave. ..." was mailed in 1909.

Oregon, a village crossroads, faced the Reading Road, which became Route 222 before the present limited-access highway was built. Wilson Bard published this view circa 1905.

The hamlet of Pequea has a picturesque setting along the Susquehanna, as seen on a card, circa 1905, published by L. B. Herr.

Main Street in Rohrerstown is now Marietta Avenue. Circa 1910, when this card was issued, a trolley ran trom Marietta to Lancaster.

Trolley tracks are clearly visible on unpaved West Main Street in Strasburg, circa 1910. Note the "Weekly News" office in the house on the right.

Main Street in Terre Hill was lined with young elm trees in 1907 when this card was mailed. Many towns had canopies of elms before the Dutch elm disease hit in the mid-20th century. Notable elms survived surrounding St. James Episcopal Church in Lancaster City well into the late 20th century.

One of the most common house forms seen in the towns of Lancaster county was the Pennsylvania German style two-front-door house. Typically, the door on the right opened into the kitchen and the one on the left into the parlor, eliminating the need for a space-wasting central hall while allowing guests to be welcomed into the best room.

John F. Ruth, early in the 20th century, was very proud of his new Queen Anne Revival-style house in Lititz. "Kind Friends," he wrote, "Here we live when you come to town call to see us." The Ruth family probably moved there from their former home in nearby Rothsville, seen in a hand-tinted card. Notice the photographer and his camera seen towards the left.

Taverns, inns and hotels are a part of Lancaster's small town landscape. The General Sutter Hotel (now Inn) was named after the Lititz-born adventurer on whose land gold was discovered in California. This 1930s card's reverse informs us that it is, "A Surprisingly Fine New Hotel situated in an Attractive Town in the Garden Spot of America" and its "30 beautifully appointed Rooms –"2.50 Up." The Black Bear in Elizabethtown houses a restaurant in 2007.

The railroad station was the heart of most prosperous small towns early in the 20th century. This circa 1905 hand-tinted view of the station at Lititz has a luggage cart in the left foreground and shows a boxcar on a siding. A replica of the 1884 structure was constructed in 1999, at the entrance to the Lititz Springs Park, where it serves as the Lititz Welcome Center.

Small town hardware stores sold a wide range of products. The Lutz store was conveniently located next to the railroad with its own siding for freight. In addition to hardware, Lutz also carried farm machinery and carriages. The Hensel Hardware Store was smaller and attached to the family home. It promoted "Seeds, Guns, Wires, Ropes" and was "Headquarters for Oliver [cast iron] Chilled Plows and STOVES."

Ephrata National Bank, Ephrata, Pa. 3113-29-N

Lancaster County has several large rural outdoor-indoor markets, with the largest being Roots and The Green Dragon (shown here). A product of the automobile age, they are open only one day a week. Especially in summer they have a carnival atmosphere. "In addition to the huge amounts of food and merchandise for sale [at the Green Dragon] each Friday, there are horse and livestock being auctioned off to the highest bidder." Roots is open on Tuesdays.

Director's Room—The Union National Mount Joy Bank, Mount Joy, Pa.

Small towns were proud of their community banks, which were often among the most impressive structures in town, as was the monumental Ephrata National Bank building seen in this 1920s view. The town banker and his board of directors were among the most prominent locals. The Director's Room in the Union National Bank in Mount Joy was a serious, formal environment.

HELEN'S COUNTRY STORE, BAINBRIDGE, LANCASTER COUNTY, PA.

Diners are a small town institution that developed with the automobile age. They evolved from lunch wagons serving factory workers. The Lyndon Diner's modern era facility in Manheim was built by DeRaffele Dining Car Company.

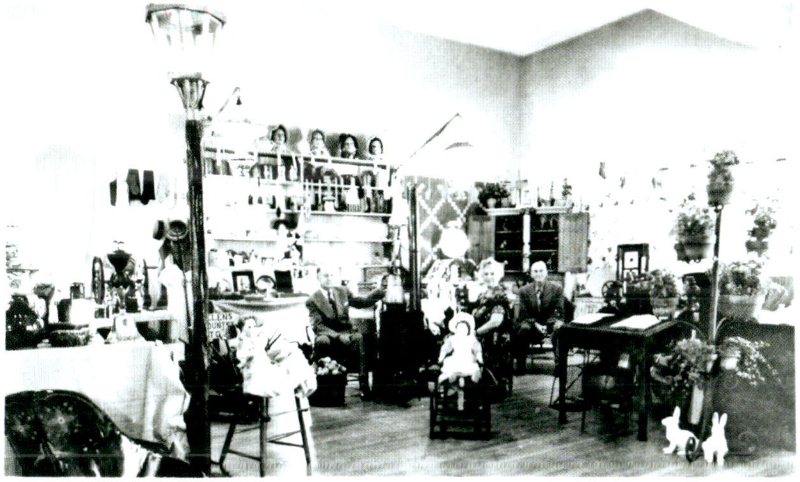

Helen's Country Store, Bainbridge, Lancaster County, Pa.

Helen's Country Store, housed in a large 19th-century house, was an antiques shop that operated in Bainbridge in the 1950s. Antiques shops are a staple of many small towns. Adamstown, in north-eastern Lancaster County, touts itself as the "Antiques Capital of America."

Photo D.B.L. 1908 OLD MENNONITE CHURCH, BUILT ABOUT [illegible], LANDISVILLE PA.

Many early local churches were built of log. The Old Mennonite Church in Landisville survived into the 20th century. It was photographed by D. B. Landis in 1908.

The Moravians, a German church with Reformation roots, founded several communities in Pennsylvania, the most successful of these included Lititz (named for Lidice in the Czech Republic), which proudly celebrates its heritage and preserves its 18th communitarian buildings, all shown in c. 1910 views. Until 1855 only Moravians could own property or live in the town. During the American Revolution the Brothers House served as a hospital, housing 450 men of whom 120 died. Linden Hall Seminary is one of the oldest schools in America devoted to educating young women. It still exists as a residential prep school.

Many small towns had "union churches," which were usually shared by two congregations – one Lutheran and one Reformed. Typically each congregation held services on alternate Sundays.

The Queen Anne Revival style mixed with Gothic touches was favored by many congregations in the late 19th century. The United Brethern Church in New Holland is pictured on a c. 1905 postcard. The 100th anniversary card for Trinity Evangelical Congregational Church of Terre Hill was issued in 1995. On the reverse we are told that "Ground breaking for the new church occurred on October 7, 1894. Cost of construction for the church was $7000. It was proudly dedicated debt free by Bishop R. Dubbs on August 4, 1895."

The interior of the Lutheran Church in Leacock and its parsonage were both typical of the early 20th century in small town Pennsylvania. The interior is unadorned except for a religious painting above the altar. The square parsonage boasted a large porch and Colonial Revival details.

Two of the principal churches in Manheim are red brick. Trinity United Evangelical Church and Zion Lutheran Church. The third large church (not pictured) housed the German Reformed congregation. Zion, also known as the "Red Rose Church," has a colorful past. The "... ground on which to build a church was conveyed to fellow Lutherans by Henry William Stiegel and his wife in 1772 – for five shillings and in the month of June yearly forever thereafter the rent of one rose if the same lawfully demanded." To this day, on the second Sunday in June a rose is ceremoniously presented to a Stiegel descendent.

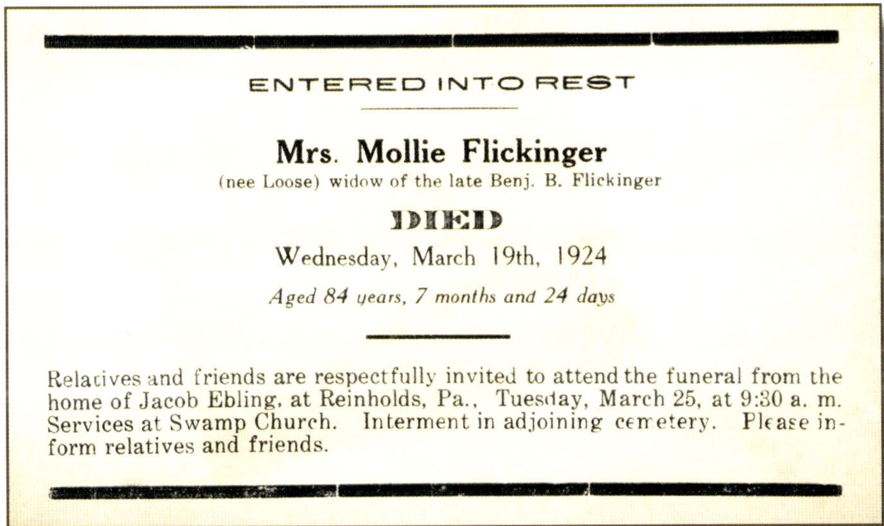

ENTERED INTO REST

Mrs. Mollie Flickinger

(nee Loose) widow of the late Benj. B. Flickinger

DIED

Wednesday, March 19th, 1924

Aged 84 years, 7 months and 24 days

Relatives and friends are respectfully invited to attend the funeral from the home of Jacob Ebling, at Reinholds, Pa., Tuesday, March 25, at 9:30 a. m. Services at Swamp Church. Interment in adjoining cemetery. Please inform relatives and friends.

Rest in peace! Many burials took place in graveyards adjoining churches. In larger towns like Columbia or Marietta park like cemeteries were often laid out on hillsides overlooking the town.

The St. Clements Campus in Ephrata, pictured in this 1920s view, continues to serve the area's Roman Catholic congregations. It adjoins Our Mother of Perpetual Help Church. The large brick building is the rectory and monastery. Other structures today provide space for a food kitchen and a homeless shelter.

Now restored and furnished with an outstanding collection of American period furniture and English accessories, the Wright's Ferry Mansion at Second and Cherry Streets in Columbia, was the home of noted intellectual and Quaker woman of affairs, Susanna Wright.

Columbia's Municipal Building at Third and Locust Streets is the remodeled remnant of the grand three-story tall 19th century Columbia Opera House, which burned in 1947.

Everybody loves a fire engine. In 1907 John a Shultz of Marietta mailed this card to a friend in Lititz. "This is a picture of our engine of our fire-department."

Millersville, settled circa 1761, was named for a prosperous local farmer, John Miller. To many the name "Millersville" today is synonymous with Millersville University, a constituent of the Pennsylvania State System of Higher Education. Established as a teacher-training school in 1855, The Millersville State Normal School is pictured in two pre-World War I views showing Old Main and the library, which was constructed in 1895 and now serves as the Biemesderfer Center.

The Columbia Hospital as it appeared in 1910, when this card was mailed to Miss Minnie L. Herr of Lancaster. The message on the back bears no relationship to the image on the front but is intriguing: "My Dear Minnie When I came home on Sun eve I ate a piece of pear butter bread … but I did sleep good." Several of Lancaster County's larger towns had their own hospitals by the early 20th century.

Elizabethtown College, affiliated with the Church of the Brethren, was founded in 1899. Written across the 1910 view of the campus is, "Dear John, Don't you think this place makes a fine home. Plenty of flowers on Campus." The school was not much larger in the 1920s when the "Aeroplane View" showing Lake Placida was made. Major growth came after World War II and today the student body number approximately 1800. The Rufus P. Buchner Meetinghouse and Young Center for Anabaptist and Pietist Groups opened overlooking the lake in 1989.

The State Hospital for Crippled Children in Elizabethtown was closed late in the late 20th century and its functions were incorporated into the Pennsylvania State University's Milton S. Hershey Medical Center in Dauphin County. On the card mailed in 1952 to a young lady in Wichita, Kansas, "Mother" writes," Left Elizabethtown this morning. Came from Harrisburg to Carlisle on Turnpike, a wonderful road. … All going well."

The Square and the Fountain at Lititz as they appeared in 1905 both with and without 4th of July decorations. Many communities decked out their town centers to celebrate Independence Day.

The Spring is the most popular feature of the park in the heart of Lititz. Three of the contemporary cards were mailed in 1910 to folks in Lancaster City. Note also that the views of the pool are identical – one is black and white, the other is in color. The difference – price.

The Masonic Homes in Elizabethtown, founded In 1910, has since morphed into the Masonic Village including community services, a children's home and a continuing care retirement community. The campus is impressive The Grand Lodge Hall, ornamented with still well-maintained formal gardens, was dedicated in 1913. The aerial view is circa. 1920. The Grand Lodge Hall Dining Room emulates the interior of an English baronial castle.

The Rest House, an out-of-doors pavilion, was a popular place for residents in summertime. The view is circa 1915.

At one time the farms at the Masonic Homes supplied most of the food eaten by residents. Much of the farming operation has been eliminated. Today the celebrated Masonic Village orchards continue the tradition supplying fruit for residents – and locals as well, who can also shop at their retail outlet.

Natural disasters are also a part of life for our small towns. The Roy Parker home on Route 441 in Washington Boro was photographed during the Susquehanna's flooding in February, 1959.

Many of our towns have war memorials. Columbia's "The Returned Solider," memorializing World War I servicemen, was dedicated in 1928. The tradition continues. Many towns have shrines to veterans of all of our wars – some right up to Iraq I.

VI. Everyday Folks

While photography was introduced into America about 1840, the early years of the 20th century marked the period when the photograph and inexpensive duplicates were widely embraced by rural families. Personal postcards, like that of the five-member John Huss family of Christiana, became all the rage. The two fashionable couples posed near a front porch and the elderly couple on a boardwalk in their garden all date from the 1905-1915 period. Of the same period is one of the author's favorite cards, which portrays a well-fed family on the front porch of their two-front-door Pennsylvania German farmhouse, no doubt, after an enormous Sunday dinner. *(continued on following page)*

Children were always prized and infants were sentimentalized, as seen in a German-printed postcard on which "Mr. NewlyWed" writes "Dr. Stork" a "$10,000,000" I.O.U. for one "pink kid." Chubby babies were preferred as most people believed that "a fat baby is a healthy baby." The studio portrait shows an infant girl sitting on a bearskin rug – a common prop of the day. The boy infant, with his hair properly parted in the middle, shares his photograph with a peegee hydrangea.

Studio portraits of kids were popular on postcards. These three cards are Lancaster County in origin and date from the early years of the 20th century. The serious girl, half sitting in the chair, is "Dorothy 4 yrs."

Cherish the ladies. "Eva Deibler," later Mrs. Alfred Bowermaster," poses on a wicker chair in her garden in the 1920s. An unidentified lady holds a bouquet of flowers, probably just picked from her garden. The picket fence behind her was common in Lancaster County in the early 20th century. Three adventurous women balance on a piece of farm machinery in a corn field.

Two girls stand in front of their two-front-door German-style farmhouse about 1910. The postcard was probably made from a family snapshot.

Two friends or, perhaps brothers posed for William Bailey, a photographer based at 36 North 3rd Street in Columbia about 1915. In the pre-Freudian age men were often photographed very cose together. On E-bay today this card would probably be offered as one of, "Two Handsome Men ... of Gay interest?"

Men: sober and otherwise. The young man in the overcoat is probably posed along the bank of the Susquehanna at an area often photographed by Lancaster County artist, Lloyd Mifflin [1846-1924]. The man with the keg under the large tree still has the strength to sit up.

Marked "George" this card belonged to George D. Landis, one of the founders of the Landis Valley Museum. Both cards are dated 1907 and postmarked in Berks County. Swimming B.A., without swim suits, was common in rural America well into the 20th century. Photographs have been published of the Landis brothers, with a friend, nude while on a camping trip along the Juniata River.

J. B. Riley was an amazing musician. It is very rare to see a one-man band that includes two string instruments. Notice the bell under his right foot. His left foot operates the drumstick.

A barber, a customer, and assistants [?] pose in front of a shop featuring a "Forepaugh and Sells Bros." circus poster for Thursday May 26 at Lancaster. The painted barber pole is highly unusual and must have been very colorful.

L. B. Herr Print **The Lancaster Tri-State Base Ball Team.**

Baseball has long been popular in Lancaster. The Lancaster Tri-States were semi-pro. The team from Bowman Technical School were student athletes. Bowman's, which lasted into the late 20th Century, was famed for training watchmakers. Lancaster's new professional ballteam, "The Barnstormers," came to town a few years ago. Their Clipper Magazine Stadium on North Prince Street has become a new landmark.

A young men's group from a rural church pose on the lawn near the cemetery. Identified on the back they include Birchard Moyer, Frank Smith, Stanford Lepley and "Myself." The view is circa 1915.

Cherry Hill School students and teacher pose for their photograph next to their building in the 1920s. Note that both Mennonite and Church children and staff are present. The neckties are a giveaway that the men and several of the boys are Church People. The photographer was "Evans Marietta Pa".

The Sunday School of Ebenezer Evangelical Congregational Church of Brownstown poses in the 1930s.

A crowd of bystanders pose for the camera in front of the Lancaster County Court House on a market day about 1910. Note the vendors wagons, sans horses, lined up along the cross-street.

You could take trolley cars from many parts of Lancaster County to Pequea, where many county residents and tourists enjoyed a ride on the miniature railroad that ran between there and York Furnace early in the 20th century.

All the world loves a parade. They occurred frequently in early 20th century central Pennsylvania. Probably Lancaster scenes, these views show some eternals of parades: a marching band, police and fire engines. Notice the fresh horse manure along the parade route in these circa 1910 views.

The young men of Wide Awake Camp, circa 1910, enjoyed their high-jinks much as today's lads do.

Descendants of the Herr family pose in front of the Hans Herr House, dated 1719, probably the oldest stone building in Lancaster County. While it was a venerated relic in 1905, it was to be many years before the building was restored to its colonial era appearance. Today it is a museum. [Also see views in Chapter VII.]

"Silver Hill," near Ephrata, was a popular excursion spot for locals early in the 20th century. They especially liked the "Stone Cave" and "Hanging Rock."

As early as 1910, when the card full of puppies was printed, cute "old-timey" postals were being sold in the county to both tourists and those nostalgic for the good old days. The same nostalgia is seen in a World War II era card when gasoline was scarce.

Disasters make popular attractions. Cars and spectators stop to see wind damage to a farm early in the 20th century.

Found in Lancaster County, this "Just Married" postcard-format photograph dating from the teens is wonderfully evocative. A placard on the door reads, "Ain't Love Grand." Note the driver in blackface, wearing a top hat.

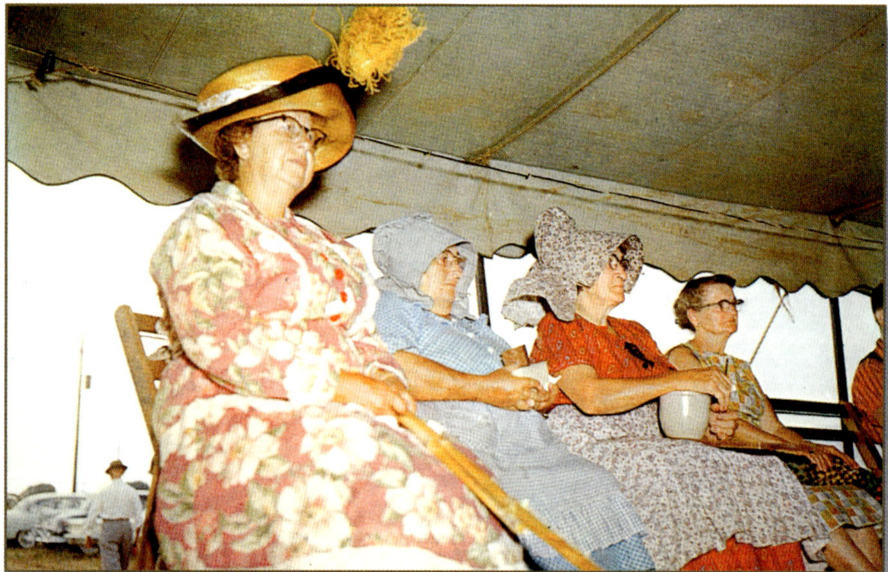

Did real Dutch women ever dress like this? On the reverse of this 1970s card, published in Mt. Joy, we read beneath a headline "Pennsylvania Dutch Garb" that we see on the front "Pennsylvania Dutch Women wearing traditional colorful costumes complete with gay hats, sunbonnets and aprons." The photograph was obviously taken at one festival or another.

Power comes, power goes. "Chief Once Mister Now," reads the banner atop this photograph located here in Lancaster County.

VII Amish and Mennonites

It is hard to believe, but the commercial exploitation of Amish images has been going on for over 100 years. These cards, both photographed by woman photographers, Frances D. Calder and Alice Malone, were copyrighted in 1906 and 1909. Note the bonnets of a type no longer worn. While children of Plain People could pose for the camera, adults could not -- hence the woman looking away from the camera.

Amish on the streets of Lancaster were fair game for photographers in the 19-teens and early -20s. The group of women were photographed along the side of the Lancaster County Courthouse, the menfolk in front of its steps. As the family walks down the street, notice the automobile and the horse-drawn delivery wagon in the background.

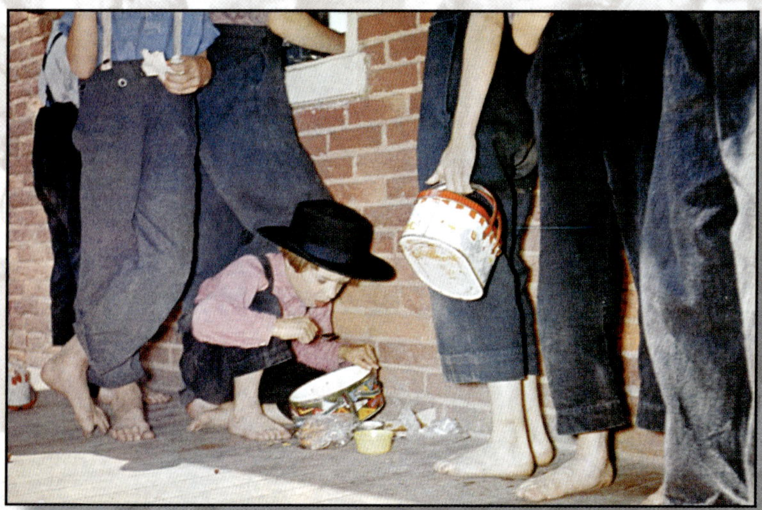

Postcards of Amish children reman popular. These 20th century pictures are designed for eye appeal. The three shot is photographed against a shingle-sheathed farmhouse with plants visible in the window. The image dates from the 1920s but was used for many years. The picture of the little boy eating his lunch surrounded by teenagers (or, at least, their lower torsos) is especially cute and dates circa 1960. It was photographed by James E. Hess of Lancaster.

"AMISH MAIDENS" reads the caption on the back. "Seven unmarried Amish girls in colorful garb walk along a rural road after Sunday worship services." This dates from the 1960s and is clearly posed. Young people and children will often pose for photographs before they are baptized. Note the change in skirt length over the years.

Amish children gather in front of a one-room schoolhouse. This long distance view was probably photographed using a telephoto lens, as Amish children rarely willingly pose at their schools.

An Amish carriage maker at work in Lancaster County, where the craft is kept alive to serve a horse-drawn society. Some carriage makers also restore historical vehicles for museums and private collectors, which explains the Conestoga Wagon in the background.

Amish are photographed at Ressler's Mill in Mascot in Lancaster County. Built in 1760 and water-powered by the Mill Creek, the Mill still grinds limited quantities of grain.

Amish youngsters in open "Courting Buggies: are popular subjects often photographed on Lancaster County's picturesque back-country roads.

Amish and covered bridges are a natural combination for a quant image. The Souderburg Bridge is one of the most photographed in the county. Spanning the Pequea Creek, the Burr type structure was built in 1885.

Shasta Industiries, which billed itself as the manufacturer of, "America's No. 1 Selling Travel Trailor" was Lancaster County-based. This circa 1960 postcard emphasizes the local connection.

Three Amish boys cheerfully pose for the camera holding tobacco leaves. Note that the boys are barefoot. Many Amish still choose to go barefoot on their farms in summer.

A mule-drawn tobacco wagon stands in front of a louvered tobacco barn on an Amish farm.

"The Amish Bank Barn." On the reverse the legend reads, "An outstanding feature of many Amish farms is the Bank Barn. A bank of ground is piled up to the second level enabling loaded wagons to be pulled into the barn at both levels."

An Amish farmer uses a three-mule hitch to plow.

Mennonite boys pose with a wagon of husked corn.

Generations of Amish farmers have had their grain ground into flour at the Ressler or Mascot Mill. (See page 106)

Amish and Old Order Mennonite men and boys harvest wheat using simple horse-drawn implements and muscle power.

"Amish Going to Market" shows a family group in a typical gray-top Lancaster County Amish buggy. More likely, the folks are going visiting on a Sunday afternoon.

The Amish love auctions. In the artist's rendition an exclusively Amish audience buys wonderful old-time stuff. In reality, the Amish and their "English" or "Gay" neighbors often compete for more mundane items.

For the outsiders, most of us, the singular Amish event is the "barn raising," celebrated on tens of thousands of postcards and in films and books.

The Hans or Christian Herr House, built in 1719, also served as a meeting house for its frontier congregation. Restored under the direction of nationally renowned restoration architect, John Milner, the Willow Street property is owned by the Lancaster Mennonite Historical Society.

Many Mennonite churches in Lancaster County have been remodeling as they adapt to change. Note how the Strasburg Mennonite Church added a Colonial Revival vestibule in the 1960s. Newly built Mennonite churches are no longer easily distinguishable from those of other denominations.

The Amish image is hard to separate from the tourist industry of Lancaster County. Many postcards combine the Amish image with the town of Intercourse (snigger, snigger). Many locals can recite a naughty limerick, or more, incorporating the names of a number of Dutchland towns including Bird-in-Hand, Intercourse, Blue Ball, and Paradise. All are in Amish territory.

The Amish also profit from the tourist industry. The miniature Amish Farm was "Handcrafted by an Old Order Amishman ... and is displayed in Rutt's Gift and Antiques Shop, Intercourse. ..." At the Old Candle Barn, "An Amish girl at work making candles ..." :at this shop "Operated by Amish" and "... open to the public [where you can] see the candles being made and take along some of the work. Specialty candles and regular candles are produced in a variety of scents." Anyone for a wedge of wax pie?

"Heart of Amishland," reads the reverse, "Amish 'horse'n buggy' and replica of an Amish couple stand at [Pennsylvania Turnpike] Exit 21 Reading-Lancaster interchange and U.S. 222. This educational exhibit acquaints visitors with Amish life as they enter PENNSYLVANIA DUTCH COUNTRY." Ain't education grand?

VIII. Tourist World

The railroad helped to make Lancaster County a tourist destination. While the Amish are featured on many early tourist pieces, other esoteric images are often seen. The view of smoking young women was mildly scandalous, as illustrated on a circa 1910 card found in Lancaster County but not identified as to origin.

The beginnings of Ephrata's Mountain Spring Hotel can be traced to a travelers tavern built as early as 1753. The hotel attained its largest size after the Civil War, in the years of the balneology craze when there was a great interest in the medicinal quality of local waters. The hotel limped along into the late 20th century in many capacities, including as a spiritualist center. Significant parts of the now being redeveloped property have been demolished.

Early hoteliers prized a location near a railroad where they could easily serve the needs of the commercial traveler as well as the vacationer. This certainly was the case at Fifes Eddy Hotel overlooking the Susquehanna at Drumore.

A number of resort hotels were sited to take advantage of views of the Susquehanna. Mailed to Maude Steigerwalt of Lancaster in 1908, but unsigned, the reverse reads: "Dearest – Am improving rapidly. Busy feeding my face, the peaches were elegant. … Will be back to the mill on Monday a week. Be good to yourself take walks regularly at noon & that will be sufficient."

"The Willows Cottages, Hotel & Restaurant" was one of the Lancaster area's earliest quality tourist accommodations. Opened years before World War II, "The Willows Motel," reads the back of one card, "is located in a most pleasant and quiet setting of old willow trees and spacious lawns in the heart of the Amish and Penna Dutch Country." Its neighborhood has changed. The Willows is now the site of the American Music Theatre right in the middle of our premier tourist strip.

The Catskills come to Lancaster County in the 1960s with the opening of the Host Farm Resort Motel "In the Land of the Hex," which featured "350 rooms, ballrooms … [a] Model Amish Farm … Color TV-every room, Penna. Dutch Tours … Hay and Sleigh Rides." Having gone through changes in ownership, the resort is still in business.

"Wheatland," Home of President James Buchanan, Lancaster, Pa. 51759-C-N

Campgrounds remain popular in the county "Hickory Run Campgrounds, Denver R.D. #2, Penna 17517 (Owned and Operated by Harvey & Alberta Musser)" offered "Ideal Campgrounds for Family Camping: Church Services – Hayrides – Boating Fishing…. Facilities include electricity – Hot Showers, Flush Toilets – Ice – Wood … (Come Visit the Penna. Dutch)"

Two of Lancaster County's many house museums were preserved thanks to the initiative of the Junior League of Lancaster. The card of "Rock Ford", the home of General Eward Hand, dates from c. 1915, long before the house became a museum (fifty years ago, from 2007). While Hand was a very prominent figure in the Revolutionary era, he did not sign the Declaration of Independence. James Buchanan's "Wheatland" is shown at the time it was acquired from private ownership in the 1930s.

Two house museums that are no more. Donegal Mills Plantation featured one of Lancaster County's very rare temple-fronted houses. The site promoted the house as "Lancaster County's Tara." The Mt. Joy area home remains in private hands as does "White Chimneys," the Slaymaker family home in Gap, which was in single-family ownership from 1720 to 1999. "Sue Slaymaker at age 5 playing in the front 1807 drawing room" was photographed by Nina Leen for a photospread published in Life Magazine in the 1960s.

Lancaster County's unique architectural treasure is the surviving buildings of the Ephrata Cloister, which was founded in 1732. Long recognized for its importance, for many years it has been a museum operated by the Pennsylvania Historical and Museum Commission. The view of the exterior of the complex was mailed in 1907 to a lady in Carlisle. The interior is a view of the kitchen in the Saron, or Sisters House.

Ephrata Cloister produced a unique body of music that is kept alive through performances of the Ephrata Cloister Chorus, which usually performs in traditional garb. The group regularly presents a musical pageant or "Vorspiel".

For many years an ever-changing number of private museums and exhibition venues have existed in Lancaster County. The Pennsylvania Dutch Farm Museum was located in Kempton. The vintage steam-powered tractor was on display at Arthur Young's at Kinzers, which for a number of years hosted a steam tractor get together.

The Strasburg Steam Railroad, "The Road to Paradise," is the oldest continuously operating short line railroad in America. Once a freight and passenger line, the railroad now primarily serves as a tourist attraction, although it still also functions as a freight railroad. It was saved from abandonment by a group of dedicated, local train buffs and still privately owned and operated. Its train station is located across the road from the Railroad Museum of Pennsylvania, consistently Lancaster County's most visited museum. Publicly owned, the Railroad Museum of Pennsylvania is operated by the Pennsylvania Historical and Museum Commission

The Landis Valley Museum is America's premier museum devoted to Pennsylvania German culture. Established by two eccentric brothers, Henry Kinzer Landis (1865-1955) and George Diller Landis (1867-1954), the "Barn Museum" opened in 1925. For many years H. K. Landis was the curator of the renamed Landis Valley Museum. The museum today is widely celebrated for its attractive buildings, extensive collections, and its many crafts exhibitions and special events, which include the springtime "Herb and Garden Faire" and autumn's "Harvest Days." Since the middle of the 20th century the museum has been operated by the Pennsylvania Historical and Museum Commission.

Car museums, all privately owned, come and go in Lancaster County. The Seiverling Antique Car and Pedal Car Museum was in Ephrata. These transient venues develop out of hobbyists' passions.

The Old Village Store in Bird-in-Hand features "… the 'shortest Covered Bridge in the world,' which connects a century-old, open-timbered barn with our 'Gay Nineties' Grocery Store. This Bridge is of 'modified Burr-truss construction – built in 1959."

"The Headquarters and Museum of the National Association of Watch and Clock Collectors, Inc.," located in Columbia, is shown before its most recent renovation in a photograph by Marshall Dussinger. "The Museum offers … a collection of clocks … which range from the Sundial to the Atomic Clock."

Mill Bridge Craft Village uses the "Museum" as an enticement to visit its sales area. "The entrance to the village," as noted on the reverse, is "from the spacious parking area [and] makes a lovely picture. Located in the center of the Amish farming country. …" It and its adjoining campground are in Soudersburg.

Dutch Haven Barn, shown in a card dated 1965, featured a "Stripping Room Gift Shop." "Stripping" is a term related to tobacco culture, not exhibitionists. The interior's restaurant features, "Penna Dutch Cooking served family style in the heart of Amish Country. Chicken pot pie, pork and sauerkraut. Amish-style turkey filing. …" It is housed in a remodeled bank barn.

One-room schoolhouses are often adapted for tourist industry uses. The Weavertown One-Room Schoolhouse, built in 1877, allows visitors to, "... re-live past school day memories with animated life-like pupils." The Olde Schoolhouse, also located on Route 340 East, features "Antiques and Other Stuff."

The Amish Farm and House is a long-lived tourist attraction on the Route 30 strip, but it is also shrinking. Because of an escalation of real estate values, it has lost its rural aspect and shares most of its site with a Target store.

Many food-related sites maintain some kind of a tourist attraction. Plain and Fancy Farm, primarily a restaurant and gift shop operation, maintains and interprets an Amish house for visitors.

Lancaster County Farm Diner in Elizabethtown was noted for the large composite rooster on its roof. High school and college pranksters prided themselves in kidnapping the bird. When the restaurant closed the rooster was sold and it now decorates a private garden.

The Julius Sturgis Pretzel House in Lititz, which opened in 1861, is the site of America's first commercial pretzel bakery.

Brownstown Restaurant in Brownstown is housed in a late 18th century tavern building. In the 20th century its specialty was attracting tourists with "... Real Penna Dutch cooking ... [and a] Home-like Atmosphere."

The Hotel Brunswick was Lancaster's premier hotel (see Chapter II) and it featured "Five Air Conditioned Restaurants" in 1950 when this card was mailed by tourists who "... had dinner & got ... [to a theatre] in time to hear Margaret Truman."

Millers Smorgasbord is still in business along Route 30 with a changing menu. In this 1966 card guests are exhorted to, "Eat Yourself Full, Leave Your Plate Empty."

Mixed metaphors abound in Dutch Country, mixing German and Holland Dutch imagery. In postcards you can see this still existing attraction growing its windmill.

The Kitchen Kettle Village in Intercourse is a major tourist attraction that grew out of a small home business making and selling local preserves and jellies.

The dinner served in the Holland Dutch Room in Dutch Haven Restaurants and Village of Shops in Soudersburg features Pennsylvania Dutch foods, including "Shoo-Fly Pie."

The Amish Village on Route 896 is the largest of the private museums devoted to depictions of Amish life and culture.

Jane and Jacob Zook's House of Crafts in Paradise featured the designs of Jacob Zook (1915-2000) "The Hex Man of Paradise." He is hanging a "Rain" sign on his sales shed. Umbrella, anyone?

Very popular souvenirs of visits to the Dutch Country are "frakturs," which are usually highly ornamented documents, often birth and baptism certificates. Sold as hand done reproductions or prints, this assortment was offered for sale by the Cloister Country Store in Ephrata.

Dutch Wonderland is a major tourist attraction. Founded by Earl Clark, it is now owned by Hershey Entertainment and Resorts, which also operates Hersheypark in Dauphin County. Its castle and monorail have become familiar Route 30 landmarks. To make room for the amusement park's expansion the Running Pump Inn, a tavern built in 1799, had to be moved to a nearby site. Note the "smoke" coming from the chimney of the stone building, in transit.

The National Wax Museum of Lancaster County Heritage stood next to Dutch Wonderland until its closing in 2007. Famed for its mechanical Amish barn raising diorama, it featured representations of many other sequences from Lancaster County History. Shown here is a day drawn from the life of Martin Chartier, a French-born fur trapper who was one of the first European settlers of Lancaster County. When the museum was sold most of its life-size mannequins were sold at public auction.

Two examples of "piggy back" enterprises to the Dutch Tourist emphasis that predated the rise of Outlet shopping along Route 30 were Terry-Town in Ephrata, which featured "towels-by-the-pound: and Famous French Galleries in Paradise ... "Where you can browse through hundreds of original oil paintings. Prices are as low as $7.50."

Lancaster's unique and exotic tourist attraction was Sweigart's Wild Animal Zoo near Ephrata, which offered wild animal performances on weekends and holidays, presided over by "Earl W. Sweigart, Host & Trainer."

Come visit Lancaster County, if you don't already live here. The hand-colored card, mailed to Miss Estella Hammon in Quarryville in 1912, bears the indistinct slogan above the couple's heads" "Receive Good Treatment." What else? Visit here. It's "YOUR TURN NEXT."

Sources and Suggestions for Additional Reading

Boyer, Dennis. *Once Upon a Hex: A Spiritual Ecology of the Pennsylvania Germans*. Oregon, Wisconsin: Badger Books, Inc. 2004.

Brener, David. *Lancaster's Gates of Heaven, Portals to the Past*. Lancaster, Pennsylvania: Temple Shaarai Shomayim, 1976.

Ellis, Franklin and Samuel Evans. *History of Lancaster County Pennsylvania*. Philadelphia: Everts and Peck, 1883.

Ensminger, Robert. *The Pennsylvania Barn: Its Origin, Evolution and Distribution*. Baltimore: The Johns Hopkins University Press, 1992.

Fegley, H. Winslow. *Farming, Always Farming*. Birdsboro, Pennsylvania: The Pennsylvania German Society, 1987.

Friesen, Steve. *A Modest Mennonite Home: The Story of the 1719 Hans Herr House*. Intercourse, Pennsylvania: Good Books, 1990.

Historic Preservation Trust of Lancaster County. *Lancaster County Architecture, 1700-1850*. Lancaster, Pennsylvania: Intelligencer Printing Company, 1992.

Johnson, Elizabeth and Craig A. Benner. *Landis Valley Museum*. Mechanicsburg, Pennsylvania: Stackpole Books, 2002.

Klein, Frederick S and Charles X. Carlson. *Old Lancaster, An Historic Pennsylvania Community from its beginnings to 1865.* Lancaster Pennsylvania: Early American Series, Inc. 1964.

Klimuska, Ed. et al. *Lancaster County*. Stillwater, Minnesota. Voyageur Press, 1998.

Kraybill, Donald. *Old Order Amish: Their Enduring Way of Life*. Baltimore: The Johns Hopkins University Press, 1993.

Lancaster New Era

Long, Amos, Jr. *The Pennsylvania German Family Farm*. Breinigsville, Pennsylvania: The Pennsylvania German Society, 1972.

Loose, John Ward Willson. *The Heritage of Lancaster*. Woodland Hills, California: Windsor Publications, Inc. 1978.

Richman, Irwin. *German Architecture in America: Folk House, Your House, Bauhaus, and More*. Atglen, Pennsylvania: Schiffer Publishing, Ltd., 2003.

___. *Pennsylvania German Farms, Gardens and Seeds: Landis Valley in Four Centuries.* Atglen, Pennsylvania: Schiffer Publishing, Ltd., 2007.

___. *The Pennsylvania Dutch Country.* Charleston, South Carolina: Arcadia Publishing, 2004.

Rineer, A Hunter. *Churches and Cemetaries of Lancaster County, Pennsylvania: A Complete Guide.* Lancaster, Pennsylvania: Lancaster County Historical Society, 1993.

Rubin, Cynthia Elyce and Morgan Williams. *Larger Than Life: The American Tall Tale Postcard, 1905-1915*. New York: Abbeville Press, 1990.

Ryan, Dorothy B. *Picture Postcards in the United States, 1893-1918*, updated ed. New York: Clarkson N. Potter, 1982.

Ryan, Thomas R., et al. *Illustrated Historical Atlas of Lancaster County*. East Petersburg, Pennsylvania, c. 2006.

Schneider, David. *Foundations in a Fertile Soil: Farming and Farm Buildings in Lancaster County Pennsylvania*. Lancaster, Pennsylvania: Historic Preservation Trust of Lancaster County, 1994.

Staff, Frank. *The Picture Postcard and Its Origins.* New York: Frederick A. Praeger, 1966.

Stranahan, Susan. *Susquehanna River of Dreams*. Baltimore: The Johns Hopkins University Press, 1993.

Stoltzfus, Louise and Jan Mast. *Lancaster County Cookbook*. Intercourse, Pennsylvania: Good Books, 1993.

Yoder, Don and Thomas E. Graves. *Pennsylvania Dutch Barn Symbols and their Meanings*. Revised and Expanded 2nd Edition. Harrisburg, Pennsylvania: Stackpole Books, 2000.

Zacher, Susan. *The Covered Bridges of Pennsylvania: A Guide*. Harrisburg, Pennsylvania: Pennsylvania Historical and Museum Commission, 1994.

Index